I0021505

SWARM Algorithm Recipes: Volume 1

Written By Richard Aragon

Table of Contents

Introduction...3
Chapter 1: Swarm Intelligence and Its Applications.. 4
Chapter 2: Reinforcement Learning and Agents.. 6
Chapter 3: SWARM Algorithms and Reinforcement Learning................................ 8
Chapter 4: General Framework and Steps for Implementing SWARM Algorithms............. 10
Swarm Optimization Algorithm (SOA)... 12
Ant Colony Optimization (ACO).. 18
Artificial Bee Colony (ABC).. 22
Slime Mold Algorithm (SMA)... 27
Firefly Algorithm (FA)... 30
Bat Algorithm (BA)... 33
Cuckoo Search (CS).. 38
Whale Optimization Algorithm (WOA)... 41
Flower Pollination Algorithm (FPA).. 44
Moth Flame Optimization (MFO)...47
Grey Wolf Optimizer (GWO)... 50
Penguin Optimization Algorithm (POA)...53
Honey Badger Optimization Algorithm (HBOA)...56
Octopus Optimization Algorithm (OOA)...59

Introduction

Swarm algorithms are a class of nature-inspired optimization techniques that mimic the collective behavior of social animals, such as ants, bees, birds, and fish. These algorithms are based on the idea that simple agents, following simple rules, can produce complex and intelligent global behavior through local interactions. Swarm algorithms have been successfully applied to solve various problems in engineering, science, and art, such as routing, scheduling, clustering, image processing, and design.

In this book, you will learn how to implement and use swarm algorithms to solve your own optimization problems. You will also discover the principles and mechanisms behind these algorithms, and how they can be adapted and improved for different scenarios. The book covers some of the most popular and widely used swarm algorithms, such as:

- Particle Swarm Optimization (PSO): An algorithm that simulates the movement of a flock of birds or a school of fish, where each particle represents a potential solution and moves towards the best position found by itself or its neighbors.
- Artificial Bee Colony (ABC): An algorithm that mimics the foraging behavior of honey bees, where each bee represents a potential solution and searches for food sources (i.e., better solutions) in the environment.
- Ant Colony Optimization (ACO): An algorithm that imitates the trail-laying and trail-following behavior of ants, where each ant represents a potential solution and builds a solution by moving from one component to another while depositing pheromone to guide other ants.
- Differential Evolution (DE): An algorithm that simulates the evolution of a population of individuals, where each individual represents a potential solution and undergoes mutation and crossover operations to generate new offspring.

The book is intended for readers who have some background in programming and mathematics, but no prior knowledge of swarm algorithms is required. The book provides pseudocode and Python code for each algorithm, along with explanations and comments. The code can be easily modified and extended to suit your own needs. The book also provides exercises and questions at the end of each chapter to help you test your understanding and practice your skills.

We hope that this book will inspire you to explore the fascinating world of swarm intelligence and unleash your creativity with swarm algorithms. Happy swarming!

Chapter 1: Swarm Intelligence and Its Applications

Swarm intelligence (SI) is a term that describes the collective behavior of decentralized, self-organized systems, natural or artificial. SI systems are typically composed of a large number of simple agents that interact locally with each other and with their environment, following simple rules or heuristics. Through these interactions, the agents can achieve global objectives or emergent properties that are not explicitly programmed or controlled by any central authority. SI systems are often inspired by natural phenomena, such as ant colonies, bee colonies, bird flocking, fish schooling, and bacterial growth.

SI has many advantages over traditional centralized or hierarchical approaches to problem-solving, such as:

- Scalability: SI systems can handle large-scale problems with many variables and constraints, as well as dynamic and uncertain environments.
- Robustness: SI systems can tolerate failures, errors, and disturbances, and can adapt to changing conditions without losing functionality.
- Flexibility: SI systems can deal with diverse and heterogeneous problems, and can incorporate new information and feedback without requiring major modifications.
- Efficiency: SI systems can exploit parallelism and distributed computation, and can use local information and communication to reduce complexity and cost.

SI has been applied to various domains and disciplines, such as engineering, science, art, and social sciences. Some examples of SI applications are:

- Optimization: SI algorithms can find optimal or near-optimal solutions to complex and nonlinear optimization problems, such as traveling salesman problem, knapsack problem, vehicle routing problem, scheduling problem, clustering problem, and network design problem.
- Data mining: SI algorithms can analyze large and complex datasets to discover patterns, trends, associations, outliers, and anomalies, such as classification, regression, feature selection, dimensionality reduction, and anomaly detection.
- Image processing: SI algorithms can process and manipulate images to enhance quality, extract information, segment objects, recognize faces, generate art, and create animations.
- Control: SI algorithms can control and coordinate the behavior of multiple agents or devices to achieve desired goals or tasks, such as swarm robotics, unmanned aerial vehicles (UAVs), smart grids, traffic management, and sensor networks.
- Design: SI algorithms can generate novel and creative designs for products, systems, architectures, artworks, and games.

- Social simulation: SI algorithms can model and simulate the behavior and dynamics of social systems and phenomena, such as opinion formation, collective decision making, group formation, social influence, cooperation, competition, conflict resolution.

Chapter 2: Reinforcement Learning and Agents

Reinforcement learning (RL) is a general framework where agents learn to perform actions in an environment so as to maximize a reward. The two main components are the environment, which represents the problem to be solved, and the agent, which represents the learning algorithm. The agent and environment continuously interact with each other. At each time step, the agent takes an action on the environment based on its policy $\pi(a_t|s_t)$, where s_t is the current observation from the environment, and receives a reward r_{t+1} and the next observation s_{t+1} from the environment. The goal is to improve the policy so as to maximize the sum of rewards (return) $G_t=\sum_{k=0}^{\infty}\gamma^k r_{t+k+1}$, where γ is a discount factor in [0,1] that discounts future rewards relative to immediate rewards. This parameter helps us focus the policy, making it care more about obtaining rewards quickly.

The environment is typically stated in the form of a Markov decision process (MDP), because many reinforcement learning algorithms for this context use dynamic programming techniques. An MDP is defined by a set of states S, a set of actions A, a transition function $P_a(s,s')=\Pr(s_{t+1}=s'|s_t=s,a_t=a)$ that specifies the probability of moving from one state to another after taking an action, and a reward function $R_a(s,s')$ that specifies the expected reward after taking an action in a state and ending up in another state. An MDP satisfies the Markov property, which means that the future state and reward depend only on the current state and action, and not on the previous history.

An agent is an entity that interacts with an environment and learns from its experience. An agent can be classified into different types based on how it learns and acts. Some of the common types of agents are:

- Value-based agents: These agents learn a value function $V(s)$ or $Q(s,a)$ that estimates how good it is to be in a state or to take an action in a state. The value function is updated based on the observed rewards and transitions. The agent then acts greedily with respect to the value function, choosing the action that maximizes the value.
- Policy-based agents: These agents learn a policy $\pi(a|s)$ that specifies what action to take in each state. The policy is updated based on the observed rewards and transitions. The agent then acts according to the policy, choosing an action with some probability.
- Actor-critic agents: These agents combine both value-based and policy-based methods. They learn both a value function and a policy, and use them to update each other. The value function acts as a critic that evaluates how good the policy is, and the policy acts as an actor that improves its actions based on the feedback from the critic.
- Model-based agents: These agents learn a model of the environment, which includes both the transition function and the reward function. The model is updated based on the observed rewards and transitions. The agent then uses the model to plan ahead and choose the best action.

Reinforcement learning algorithms can be categorized into different types based on how they balance exploration and exploitation. Exploration is when the agent tries new actions that may lead to better outcomes in the future, while exploitation is when the agent uses its current knowledge to choose the best action for immediate reward. Some of the common types of algorithms are:

- On-policy algorithms: These algorithms learn about and act on the same policy. They explore by choosing random actions with some probability (e.g., ϵ-greedy) or by adding some noise to their actions (e.g., Gaussian noise). Examples of on-policy algorithms are SARSA, REINFORCE, A2C.
- Off-policy algorithms: These algorithms learn about one policy while acting on another policy. They explore by using a behavior policy that is different from the target policy that they want to improve. Examples of off-policy algorithms are Q-learning, DQN, DDPG.
- Monte Carlo methods: These methods learn from complete episodes or trajectories of experience. They update their estimates based on the average return obtained from each episode. They do not require a model of the environment or bootstrapping from other estimates.
- Temporal difference methods: These methods learn from incomplete episodes or partial trajectories of experience. They update their estimates based on the difference between their current estimate and a target estimate that is obtained from one-step lookahead or multi-step lookahead. They can use a model of the environment or bootstrapping from other estimates.

In this chapter, we have introduced the basic concepts and terminology of reinforcement learning and agents. We have also discussed some of the common types and characteristics of agents and algorithms. In the next chapter, we will present the general framework and steps for implementing reinforcement learning algorithms.

Chapter 3: SWARM Algorithms and Reinforcement Learning

SWARM algorithms are a class of reinforcement learning algorithms that use multiple agents to solve complex and dynamic problems. SWARM algorithms are inspired by the collective behavior of natural swarms, such as ants, bees, birds, and fish, that can achieve global objectives through local interactions and coordination. SWARM algorithms combine the advantages of swarm intelligence and reinforcement learning, such as scalability, robustness, flexibility, efficiency, exploration, and exploitation.

SWARM algorithms can be seen as an extension of reinforcement learning to multi-agent systems, where each agent has its own state, action, policy, and reward. However, unlike traditional multi-agent reinforcement learning, where the agents are usually heterogeneous and have different goals or roles, SWARM algorithms assume that the agents are homogeneous and have the same goal or role. Moreover, SWARM algorithms do not require explicit communication or coordination among the agents, but rather rely on implicit information exchange through the environment or the behavior of other agents.

SWARM algorithms can be categorized into different types based on how they use swarm intelligence principles and mechanisms to enhance reinforcement learning. Some of the common types of SWARM algorithms are:

- Particle Swarm Reinforcement Learning (PSRL): These algorithms use particle swarm optimization to update the policies or value functions of the agents. Each agent represents a particle in the swarm, and moves towards the best position found by itself or its neighbors. The position of a particle corresponds to a policy or a value function, and the fitness of a position corresponds to the expected return of a policy or a value function. Examples of PSRL algorithms are PSO-Q[1], PSO-R[2], and PSO-AC[3].
- Artificial Bee Colony Reinforcement Learning (ABCRL): These algorithms use artificial bee colony optimization to update the policies or value functions of the agents. Each agent represents a bee in the colony, and searches for food sources in the environment. A food source corresponds to a policy or a value function, and the quality of a food source corresponds to the expected return of a policy or a value function. Examples of ABCRL algorithms are ABC-Q[4], ABC-R[5], and ABC-AC[6].
- Ant Colony Reinforcement Learning (ACRL): These algorithms use ant colony optimization to update the policies or value functions of the agents. Each agent represents an ant in the colony, and builds a solution by moving from one component to another while depositing pheromone to guide other ants. A component corresponds to an action or a state-action pair, and the amount of pheromone on a component corresponds to the expected return of an action or a state-action pair. Examples of ACRL algorithms are ACO-Q, ACO-R, and ACO-AC.
- Differential Evolution Reinforcement Learning (DERL): These algorithms use differential evolution to update the policies or value functions of the agents. Each agent represents

an individual in the population, and undergoes mutation and crossover operations to generate new offspring. An individual corresponds to a policy or a value function, and the fitness of an individual corresponds to the expected return of a policy or a value function. Examples of DERL algorithms are DE-Q, DE-R, and DE-AC.

In this chapter, we have introduced the basic concepts and terminology of SWARM algorithms and reinforcement learning. We have also discussed some of the common types and characteristics of SWARM algorithms. In the next chapter, we will present the general framework and steps for implementing SWARM algorithms.

Chapter 4: General Framework and Steps for Implementing SWARM Algorithms

SWARM algorithms are a class of reinforcement learning algorithms that use multiple agents to solve complex and dynamic problems. SWARM algorithms are inspired by the collective behavior of natural swarms, such as ants, bees, birds, and fish, that can achieve global objectives through local interactions and coordination. In this chapter, we will present the general framework and steps for implementing SWARM algorithms.

The general framework of SWARM algorithms consists of four main components: the problem, the environment, the agents, and the algorithm. The problem is the optimization task that we want to solve using SWARM algorithms. The environment is the representation of the problem in terms of states, actions, rewards, and transitions. The agents are the learning entities that interact with the environment and each other to find the optimal solution. The algorithm is the procedure that guides the agents to update their policies or value functions based on their experience.

The general steps for implementing SWARM algorithms are as follows:

1. Define the problem: The first step is to define the problem that we want to solve using SWARM algorithms. We need to specify the objective function that we want to minimize or maximize, the constraints that we need to satisfy, and the variables that we need to optimize.
2. Model the environment: The second step is to model the environment that represents the problem. We need to define the set of states that describe the possible configurations of the variables, the set of actions that describe the possible changes of the variables, the reward function that describes the immediate feedback for each state-action pair, and the transition function that describes the probability of moving from one state to another after taking an action.
3. Initialize the agents: The third step is to initialize the agents that will interact with the environment and each other. We need to define the number of agents, their initial positions or policies or value functions, their parameters such as learning rate, exploration rate, inertia weight, etc., and their roles such as particle, bee, ant, individual, etc.
4. Execute the algorithm: The fourth step is to execute the algorithm that guides the agents to update their positions or policies or value functions based on their experience. We need to define the termination criterion such as maximum number of iterations or minimum error threshold, and then repeat the following steps until the termination criterion is met:
    - For each agent:
        - Observe the current state from the environment
        - Select an action based on its position or policy or value function
        - Execute the action on the environment

Chapter 4: General Framework and Steps for Implementing SWARM Algorithms

SWARM algorithms are a class of reinforcement learning algorithms that use multiple agents to solve complex and dynamic problems. SWARM algorithms are inspired by the collective behavior of natural swarms, such as ants, bees, birds, and fish, that can achieve global objectives through local interactions and coordination. In this chapter, we will present the general framework and steps for implementing SWARM algorithms.

The general framework of SWARM algorithms consists of four main components: the problem, the environment, the agents, and the algorithm. The problem is the optimization task that we want to solve using SWARM algorithms. The environment is the representation of the problem in terms of states, actions, rewards, and transitions. The agents are the learning entities that interact with the environment and each other to find the optimal solution. The algorithm is the procedure that guides the agents to update their policies or value functions based on their experience.

The general steps for implementing SWARM algorithms are as follows:

1. Define the problem: The first step is to define the problem that we want to solve using SWARM algorithms. We need to specify the objective function that we want to minimize or maximize, the constraints that we need to satisfy, and the variables that we need to optimize.
2. Model the environment: The second step is to model the environment that represents the problem. We need to define the set of states that describe the possible configurations of the variables, the set of actions that describe the possible changes of the variables, the reward function that describes the immediate feedback for each state-action pair, and the transition function that describes the probability of moving from one state to another after taking an action.
3. Initialize the agents: The third step is to initialize the agents that will interact with the environment and each other. We need to define the number of agents, their initial positions or policies or value functions, their parameters such as learning rate, exploration rate, inertia weight, etc., and their roles such as particle, bee, ant, individual, etc.
4. Execute the algorithm: The fourth step is to execute the algorithm that guides the agents to update their positions or policies or value functions based on their experience. We need to define the termination criterion such as maximum number of iterations or minimum error threshold, and then repeat the following steps until the termination criterion is met:
   - For each agent:
     - Observe the current state from the environment
     - Select an action based on its position or policy or value function
     - Execute the action on the environment

an individual in the population, and undergoes mutation and crossover operations to generate new offspring. An individual corresponds to a policy or a value function, and the fitness of an individual corresponds to the expected return of a policy or a value function. Examples of DERL algorithms are DE-Q, DE-R, and DE-AC.

In this chapter, we have introduced the basic concepts and terminology of SWARM algorithms and reinforcement learning. We have also discussed some of the common types and characteristics of SWARM algorithms. In the next chapter, we will present the general framework and steps for implementing SWARM algorithms.

- Observe the next state and reward from the environment
- Update its position or policy or value function based on its own experience and/or other agents' experience
  - Evaluate the performance of the agents by calculating their fitness values or expected returns
  - Record or display the best solution found so far

5. Analyze the results: The final step is to analyze the results obtained by executing the algorithm. We need to evaluate how well the algorithm solved the problem by comparing its performance with other methods or benchmarks, and by analyzing its convergence behavior, robustness, scalability, etc.

In this chapter, we have presented the general framework and steps for implementing SWARM algorithms. In the following chapters, we will describe in detail the most popular and widely used SWARM algorithms.

Swarm Optimization Algorithm (SOA)

- The 'ingredients' for the algorithm in the Recipe:
  - A population of agents (or particles) that can move in a multidimensional search space
  - A fitness function that evaluates the quality of each agent's position
  - A communication protocol that allows agents to share information with their neighbors
  - A set of parameters that control the exploration and exploitation trade-off

- An example of the recipe once it is 'cooked':
  - The SOA can be used to find the optimal solution to a complex optimization problem, such as minimizing a nonlinear function or designing a neural network
  - The SOA starts with a random initialization of the agents' positions and velocities
  - At each iteration, each agent evaluates its fitness and compares it with its best known position (personal best) and the best known position among its neighbors (global best)
  - Based on these comparisons, each agent updates its velocity and position using a stochastic formula that balances exploration and exploitation
  - The algorithm terminates when a predefined criterion is met, such as reaching a maximum number of iterations or achieving a desired fitness value

- A pseudocode Python example of the Recipe:

Python
```python
# Import numpy for numerical operations
import numpy as np

# Define the fitness function (example: Rastrigin function)
def fitness(x):
    return 10 * len(x) + np.sum(x**2 - 10 * np.cos(2 * np.pi * x))

# Define the parameters of the SOA
n_agents = 100 # Number of agents
n_dims = 10 # Number of dimensions
max_iter = 1000 # Maximum number of iterations
w = 0.9 # Inertia weight
```

```python
c1 = 2 # Cognitive coefficient
c2 = 2 # Social coefficient
lb = -5.12 # Lower bound of the search space
ub = 5.12 # Upper bound of the search space

# Initialize the agents' positions and velocities randomly
positions = np.random.uniform(lb, ub, (n_agents, n_dims))
velocities = np.random.uniform(-1, 1, (n_agents, n_dims))

# Initialize the personal best positions and fitness values
pbest_positions = positions.copy()
pbest_fitness = np.array([fitness(x) for x in pbest_positions])

# Initialize the global best position and fitness value
gbest_position = pbest_positions[np.argmin(pbest_fitness)]
gbest_fitness = np.min(pbest_fitness)

# Main loop of the SOA
for i in range(max_iter):
 # Update the velocities and positions of each agent
 for j in range(n_agents):
  # Generate two random numbers between 0 and 1
  r1 = np.random.rand()
  r2 = np.random.rand()

  # Update the velocity using the SOA formula
  velocities[j] = w * velocities[j] + c1 * r1 * (pbest_positions[j] -
positions[j]) + c2 * r2 * (gbest_position - positions[j])

  # Update the position by adding the velocity
  positions[j] = positions[j] + velocities[j]

  # Apply boundary conditions (clip the position to the search
space)
  positions[j] = np.clip(positions[j], lb, ub)

  # Evaluate the fitness of the new position
```

```python
        f = fitness(positions[j])

        # Update the personal best position and fitness if improved
        if f < pbest_fitness[j]:
         pbest_positions[j] = positions[j].copy()
         pbest_fitness[j] = f

         # Update the global best position and fitness if improved
         if f < gbest_fitness:
          gbest_position = pbest_positions[j].copy()
          gbest_fitness = f

    # Print the iteration number and the global best fitness value
    print(f"Iteration {i+1}: Global best fitness =
{gbest_fitness:.4f}")

# Print the final result
print(f"Final result: Global best position = {gbest_position}, Global
best fitness = {gbest_fitness:.4f}")
```

Particle Swarm Optimization (PSO)

- The 'ingredients' for the algorithm in the Recipe:
  - A population of particles that can move in a multidimensional search space
  - A fitness function that evaluates the quality of each particle's position
  - A velocity update rule that incorporates the particle's personal best position, the global best position, and a random factor
  - A set of parameters that control the inertia, cognitive, and social components of the velocity update rule

- An example of the recipe once it is 'cooked':
  - The PSO can be used to find the optimal solution to a complex optimization problem, such as training a neural network or tuning a controller
  - The PSO starts with a random initialization of the particles' positions and velocities
  - At each iteration, each particle evaluates its fitness and compares it with its personal best position and the global best position
  - Based on these comparisons, each particle updates its velocity and position using a stochastic formula that balances exploration and exploitation
  - The algorithm terminates when a predefined criterion is met, such as reaching a maximum number of iterations or achieving a desired fitness value

- A pseudocode Python example of the Recipe:

```Python
# Import numpy for numerical operations
import numpy as np

# Define the fitness function (example: Rosenbrock function)
def fitness(x):
  return np.sum(100 * (x[1:] - x[:-1]**2)**2 + (1 - x[:-1])**2)

# Define the parameters of the PSO
n_particles = 100 # Number of particles
n_dims = 10 # Number of dimensions
max_iter = 1000 # Maximum number of iterations
w = 0.9 # Inertia weight
c1 = 2 # Cognitive coefficient
```

```python
c2 = 2 # Social coefficient
lb = -5 # Lower bound of the search space
ub = 5 # Upper bound of the search space

# Initialize the particles' positions and velocities randomly
positions = np.random.uniform(lb, ub, (n_particles, n_dims))
velocities = np.random.uniform(-1, 1, (n_particles, n_dims))

# Initialize the personal best positions and fitness values
pbest_positions = positions.copy()
pbest_fitness = np.array([fitness(x) for x in pbest_positions])

# Initialize the global best position and fitness value
gbest_position = pbest_positions[np.argmin(pbest_fitness)]
gbest_fitness = np.min(pbest_fitness)

# Main loop of the PSO
for i in range(max_iter):
 # Update the velocities and positions of each particle
 for j in range(n_particles):
  # Generate two random numbers between 0 and 1
  r1 = np.random.rand()
  r2 = np.random.rand()

  # Update the velocity using the PSO formula
  velocities[j] = w * velocities[j] + c1 * r1 * (pbest_positions[j] -
positions[j]) + c2 * r2 * (gbest_position - positions[j])

  # Update the position by adding the velocity
  positions[j] = positions[j] + velocities[j]

  # Apply boundary conditions (clip the position to the search
space)
  positions[j] = np.clip(positions[j], lb, ub)

  # Evaluate the fitness of the new position
  f = fitness(positions[j])
```

```python
    # Update the personal best position and fitness if improved
    if f < pbest_fitness[j]:
      pbest_positions[j] = positions[j].copy()
      pbest_fitness[j] = f

      # Update the global best position and fitness if improved
      if f < gbest_fitness:
        gbest_position = pbest_positions[j].copy()
        gbest_fitness = f

  # Print the iteration number and the global best fitness value
  print(f"Iteration {i+1}: Global best fitness =
{gbest_fitness:.4f}")

# Print the final result
print(f"Final result: Global best position = {gbest_position}, Global
best fitness = {gbest_fitness:.4f}")
```

Ant Colony Optimization (ACO)

- The 'ingredients' for the algorithm in the Recipe:
  - A set of artificial ants that can explore a discrete search space
  - A pheromone matrix that stores the amount of pheromone deposited on each edge of the search space
  - A heuristic function that guides the ants towards promising regions of the search space
  - A set of parameters that control the pheromone evaporation, intensification, and diversification

- An example of the recipe once it is 'cooked':
  - The ACO can be used to find the optimal solution to a combinatorial optimization problem, such as the traveling salesman problem or the vehicle routing problem
  - The ACO starts with a random initialization of the ants' positions and pheromone matrix
  - At each iteration, each ant constructs a solution by moving from one node to another according to a probabilistic rule that depends on the pheromone and heuristic values
  - After all ants have completed their solutions, the pheromone matrix is updated by evaporating some pheromone and depositing more pheromone on the edges that belong to the best solutions
  - The algorithm terminates when a predefined criterion is met, such as reaching a maximum number of iterations or finding a satisfactory solution

- A pseudocode Python example of the Recipe:

Python
```python
# Import numpy for numerical operations
import numpy as np

# Define the fitness function (example: traveling salesman
problem)
def fitness(solution):
 # Calculate the total distance of a tour
 distance = 0
 for i in range(len(solution)):
```

```python
        # Get the current and next city index
        current_city = solution[i]
        next_city = solution[(i+1) % len(solution)]

        # Get the distance between the two cities
        distance += distances[current_city][next_city]

    return distance

# Define the parameters of the ACO
n_ants = 10 # Number of ants
n_cities = 20 # Number of cities
max_iter = 1000 # Maximum number of iterations
alpha = 1 # Pheromone importance factor
beta = 2 # Heuristic importance factor
rho = 0.1 # Pheromone evaporation rate
Q = 100 # Pheromone deposit factor

# Generate a random symmetric matrix of distances between cities
distances = np.random.randint(1, 100, (n_cities, n_cities))
distances = (distances + distances.T) / 2

# Initialize the pheromone matrix with a small positive value
pheromones = np.ones((n_cities, n_cities))

# Main loop of the ACO
for i in range(max_iter):
    # Initialize an empty list of solutions
    solutions = []

    # Loop over each ant
    for j in range(n_ants):
        # Initialize an empty solution
        solution = []

        # Choose a random starting city
        start_city = np.random.randint(n_cities)
```

```python
    # Add the starting city to the solution
    solution.append(start_city)

    # Loop until all cities are visited
    while len(solution) < n_cities:
      # Get the current city index
      current_city = solution[-1]

      # Calculate the probabilities for moving to each city
(excluding already visited ones)
      probabilities = []
      for k in range(n_cities):
        if k not in solution:
          # Calculate the probability using the pheromone and
heuristic values
          probability = (pheromones[current_city][k] ** alpha) * ((1 /
distances[current_city][k]) ** beta)
          probabilities.append(probability)
        else:
          # Assign zero probability to already visited cities
          probabilities.append(0)

      # Normalize the probabilities to sum up to one
      probabilities = probabilities / np.sum(probabilities)

      # Choose the next city using roulette wheel selection
      next_city = np.random.choice(n_cities, p=probabilities)

      # Add the next city to the solution
      solution.append(next_city)

    # Add the solution to the list of solutions
    solutions.append(solution)

  # Evaluate the fitness of each solution
  fitness_values = np.array([fitness(s) for s in solutions])
```

```python
    # Find the best solution and its fitness value
    best_solution = solutions[np.argmin(fitness_values)]
    best_fitness = np.min(fitness_values)

    # Update the pheromone matrix by evaporating some pheromone and
    depositing more pheromone on the edges that belong to the best
    solution
    for l in range(n_cities):
      for m in range(n_cities):
        # Evaporate some pheromone
        pheromones[l][m] = (1 - rho) * pheromones[l][m]

        # Deposit more pheromone if the edge belongs to the best
    solution
        if (l in best_solution) and (m ==
    best_solution[(best_solution.index(l) + 1) % n_cities]):
          pheromones[l][m] += Q / best_fitness

    # Print the iteration number and the best fitness value
    print(f"Iteration {i+1}: Best fitness = {best_fitness:.4f}")

    # Print the final result
    print(f"Final result: Best solution = {best_solution}, Best fitness =
    {best_fitness:.4f}")
```

Artificial Bee Colony (ABC)

- The 'ingredients' for the algorithm in the Recipe:
  - A population of artificial bees that can explore a continuous search space
  - A food source matrix that stores the position and fitness value of each food source (a potential solution)
  - A selection mechanism that assigns different roles to the bees (employed, onlooker, or scout) and determines their probability of choosing a food source
  - A perturbation operator that generates a new position for a bee by using a randomly chosen neighbor
  - A set of parameters that control the size of the population, the number of food sources, and the limit of trials for abandoning a food source

- An example of the recipe once it is 'cooked':
  - The ABC can be used to find the optimal solution to a complex optimization problem, such as clustering data or scheduling tasks
  - The ABC starts with a random initialization of the food source matrix
  - At each iteration, each employed bee evaluates its assigned food source and generates a new position by applying the perturbation operator
  - If the new position has a better fitness value than the old one, the bee replaces its food source with the new one and resets its trial counter; otherwise, it keeps its food source and increments its trial counter
  - After all employed bees have completed their search, they share their information with the onlooker bees
  - Each onlooker bee chooses a food source probabilistically based on its fitness value and performs a similar search as the employed bees
  - After all onlooker bees have completed their search, a scout bee is selected from the employed bees that have reached the limit of trials
  - The scout bee abandons its food source and randomly generates a new one
  - The algorithm terminates when a predefined criterion is met, such as reaching a maximum number of iterations or achieving a desired fitness value

- A pseudocode Python example of the Recipe:

```python
# Import numpy for numerical operations
import numpy as np
```

```python
# Define the fitness function (example: Ackley function)
def fitness(x):
 return -20 * np.exp(-0.2 * np.sqrt(0.5 * np.sum(x**2))) - np.exp(0.5
* np.sum(np.cos(2 * np.pi * x))) + np.e + 20

# Define the parameters of the ABC
n_bees = 100 # Number of bees
n_dims = 10 # Number of dimensions
max_iter = 1000 # Maximum number of iterations
n_food = n_bees // 2 # Number of food sources
limit = 100 # Limit of trials for abandoning a food source
lb = -5 # Lower bound of the search space
ub = 5 # Upper bound of the search space

# Initialize the food source matrix randomly
food_matrix = np.random.uniform(lb, ub, (n_food, n_dims + 2))

# Evaluate the fitness value of each food source and initialize
the trial counter to zero
for i in range(n_food):
 food_matrix[i][-2] = fitness(food_matrix[i][:-2])
 food_matrix[i][-1] = 0

# Main loop of the ABC
for j in range(max_iter):
 # Loop over each employed bee
 for k in range(n_food):
  # Choose a random neighbor index (different from k)
  neighbor = k
  while neighbor == k:
   neighbor = np.random.randint(n_food)

  # Choose a random dimension index
  dim = np.random.randint(n_dims)

  # Generate a new position by applying the perturbation operator
  new_position = food_matrix[k][:-2].copy()
```

```python
    new_position[dim] = new_position[dim] + np.random.uniform(-1, 1) *
(new_position[dim] - food_matrix[neighbor][dim])

    # Apply boundary conditions (clip the position to the search
space)
    new_position[dim] = np.clip(new_position[dim], lb, ub)

    # Evaluate the fitness value of the new position
    new_fitness = fitness(new_position)

    # Compare the new fitness with the old one and update
accordingly
    if new_fitness < food_matrix[k][-2]:
    # Replace the old position with the new one and reset the
trial counter
        food_matrix[k][:-2] = new_position.copy()
        food_matrix[k][-2] = new_fitness
        food_matrix[k][-1] = 0
    else:
    # Increment the trial counter
        food_matrix[k][-1] += 1

# Calculate the probability of choosing each food source by the
onlooker bees based on its fitness value
probabilities = np.array([1 / (1 + f) for f in food_matrix[:, -2]])
probabilities = probabilities / np.sum(probabilities)

# Loop over each onlooker bee
for l in range(n_food):
# Choose a food source probabilistically
food = np.random.choice(n_food, p=probabilities)

# Choose a random neighbor index (different from food)
neighbor = food
while neighbor == food:
    neighbor = np.random.randint(n_food)
```

```python
    # Replace the old position and concentration with the new ones
    positions[j] = new_position.copy()
    concentrations[j] = new_concentration

    # Find the best slime mold and its fitness value
    best_slime = np.argmin([fitness(p) for p in positions])
    best_fitness = fitness(positions[best_slime])

    # Print the iteration number and the best fitness value
    print(f"Iteration {i+1}: Best fitness = {best_fitness:.4f}")

# Print the final result
print(f"Final result: Best solution = {positions[best_slime]}, Best
fitness = {best_fitness:.4f}")
```

Firefly Algorithm (FA)

- The 'ingredients' for the algorithm in the Recipe:
    - A population of fireflies that can move in a continuous search space
    - A brightness function that evaluates the quality of each firefly's position
    - A light intensity function that determines how attractive a firefly is to other fireflies
    - A set of parameters that control the initial light intensity, the light absorption coefficient, and the randomization factor

- An example of the recipe once it is 'cooked':
    - The FA can be used to find the optimal solution to a complex optimization problem, such as feature selection or function optimization
    - The FA starts with a random initialization of the fireflies' positions and brightness values
    - At each iteration, each firefly compares its brightness with other fireflies and moves towards a brighter firefly if it exists
    - The movement of a firefly is influenced by the light intensity, which decreases as the distance between fireflies increases, and by a random factor, which introduces some variability
    - The algorithm terminates when a predefined criterion is met, such as reaching a maximum number of iterations or achieving a desired solution quality

- A pseudocode Python example of the Recipe:

Python
```python
# Import numpy for numerical operations
import numpy as np

# Define the fitness function (example: Griewank function)
def fitness(x):
  return 1 + np.sum(x**2 / 4000) - np.prod(np.cos(x /
np.sqrt(np.arange(1, len(x) + 1))))

# Define the parameters of the FA
n_fireflies = 100 # Number of fireflies
n_dims = 10 # Number of dimensions
max_iter = 1000 # Maximum number of iterations
```

```python
I0 = 1 # Initial light intensity
gamma = 0.5 # Light absorption coefficient
alpha = 0.2 # Randomization factor
lb = -10 # Lower bound of the search space
ub = 10 # Upper bound of the search space

# Initialize the firefly positions and brightness values randomly
positions = np.random.uniform(lb, ub, (n_fireflies, n_dims))
brightness = np.array([fitness(x) for x in positions])

# Main loop of the FA
for i in range(max_iter):
 # Loop over each firefly
 for j in range(n_fireflies):
  # Loop over each other firefly
  for k in range(n_fireflies):
   # Check if the other firefly is brighter than the current one
   if brightness[k] < brightness[j]:
    # Calculate the distance between the two fireflies
    distance = np.linalg.norm(positions[j] - positions[k])

    # Calculate the light intensity at the current firefly
position
    intensity = I0 * np.exp(-gamma * distance**2)

    # Generate a new position by moving towards the brighter
firefly and adding some randomness
    new_position = positions[j] + intensity * (positions[k] -
positions[j]) + alpha * (np.random.uniform(-1, 1, n_dims) - 0.5)

    # Apply boundary conditions (clip the position to the search
space)
    new_position = np.clip(new_position, lb, ub)

    # Evaluate the fitness value of the new position
    new_fitness = fitness(new_position)
```

```python
    # Compare the new fitness with the old one and update
accordingly
    if new_fitness < brightness[j]:
      # Replace the old position and brightness with the new ones
      positions[j] = new_position.copy()
      brightness[j] = new_fitness

  # Find the best firefly and its fitness value
  best_firefly = np.argmin(brightness)
  best_fitness = np.min(brightness)

  # Print the iteration number and the best fitness value
  print(f"Iteration {i+1}: Best fitness = {best_fitness:.4f}")

# Print the final result
print(f"Final result: Best solution = {positions[best_firefly]},
Best fitness = {best_fitness:.4f}")
```

Bat Algorithm (BA)

- The 'ingredients' for the algorithm in the Recipe:
  - A population of bats that can fly in a continuous search space
  - A frequency function that determines how fast each bat changes its position
  - A loudness function that determines how likely each bat is to generate a new solution
  - A pulse rate function that determines how likely each bat is to exploit the best solution
  - A set of parameters that control the frequency range, the loudness reduction, and the pulse rate increase

- An example of the recipe once it is 'cooked':
  - The BA can be used to find the optimal solution to a complex optimization problem, such as multimodal functions or engineering design
  - The BA starts with a random initialization of the bats' positions, frequencies, loudness values, and pulse rates
  - At each iteration, each bat updates its frequency, velocity, and position by applying the frequency function and following the best solution
  - Each bat generates a new solution by adding some randomness to its current position and evaluates its fitness value
  - If the new solution is better than the old one and a random number is less than the loudness value, the bat accepts the new solution and updates its loudness and pulse rate values
  - If a random number is less than the pulse rate value, the bat generates another new solution by exploiting the best solution and evaluates its fitness value
  - If the new solution is better than the old one and a random number is less than the loudness value, the bat accepts the new solution and updates its loudness and pulse rate values
  - The algorithm terminates when a predefined criterion is met, such as reaching a maximum number of iterations or achieving a desired solution quality

- A pseudocode Python example of the Recipe:

```python
# Import numpy for numerical operations
import numpy as np
```

```python
# Define the fitness function (example: Schwefel function)
def fitness(x):
  return 418.9829 * len(x) - np.sum(x * np.sin(np.sqrt(np.abs(x))))

# Define the parameters of the BA
n_bats = 100 # Number of bats
n_dims = 10 # Number of dimensions
max_iter = 1000 # Maximum number of iterations
f_min = 0 # Minimum frequency
f_max = 1 # Maximum frequency
A0 = 1 # Initial loudness
alpha = 0.9 # Loudness reduction factor
r0 = 0.5 # Initial pulse rate
gamma = 0.9 # Pulse rate increase factor
lb = -500 # Lower bound of the search space
ub = 500 # Upper bound of the search space

# Initialize the bat positions, velocities, frequencies, loudness
values, and pulse rates randomly
positions = np.random.uniform(lb, ub, (n_bats, n_dims))
velocities = np.zeros((n_bats, n_dims))
frequencies = np.random.uniform(f_min, f_max, n_bats)
loudness = np.ones(n_bats) * A0
pulse_rates = np.ones(n_bats) * r0

# Evaluate the fitness value of each bat position
fitness_values = np.array([fitness(x) for x in positions])

# Find the best bat position and its fitness value
best_position = positions[np.argmin(fitness_values)]
best_fitness = np.min(fitness_values)

# Main loop of the BA
for i in range(max_iter):
 # Loop over each bat
 for j in range(n_bats):
  # Update the frequency by applying the frequency function
```

```python
    frequencies[j] = f_min + (f_max - f_min) * np.random.rand()

    # Update the velocity by adding the product of frequency and
distance to best position
    velocities[j] = velocities[j] + (positions[j] - best_position) *
frequencies[j]

    # Update the position by adding the velocity
    positions[j] = positions[j] + velocities[j]

    # Apply boundary conditions (clip the position to the search
space)
    positions[j] = np.clip(positions[j], lb, ub)

    # Generate a new position by adding some randomness to current
position
    new_position = positions[j] + np.random.uniform(-1, 1, n_dims)

    # Apply boundary conditions (clip the new position to the
search space)
    new_position = np.clip(new_position, lb, ub)

    # Evaluate the fitness value of the new position
    new_fitness = fitness(new_position)

    # Compare the new fitness with the old one and update
accordingly if a random number is less than loudness value
    if (new_fitness < fitness_values[j]) and (np.random.rand() <
loudness[j]):
        # Replace the old position and fitness with the new ones
        positions[j] = new_position.copy()
        fitness_values[j] = new_fitness

        # Update the loudness and pulse rate values
        loudness[j] = alpha * loudness[j]
        pulse_rates[j] = r0 * (1 - np.exp(-gamma * i))
```

```python
    # Update the best position and fitness if improved
    if new_fitness < best_fitness:
     best_position = positions[j].copy()
     best_fitness = new_fitness


   # Generate another new position by exploiting the best position
if a random number is less than pulse rate value
   if np.random.rand() < pulse_rates[j]:
    # Generate a new position by adding some randomness to best
position
    new_position = best_position + np.random.uniform(-1, 1, n_dims) *
loudness[j]

    # Apply boundary conditions (clip the new position to the
search space)
    new_position = np.clip(new_position, lb, ub)

    # Evaluate the fitness value of the new position
    new_fitness = fitness(new_position)

    # Compare the new fitness with the old one and update
accordingly if a random number is less than loudness value
    if (new_fitness < fitness_values[j]) and (np.random.rand() <
loudness[j]):
     # Replace the old position and fitness with the new ones
     positions[j] = new_position.copy()
     fitness_values[j] = new_fitness

     # Update the loudness and pulse rate values
     loudness[j] = alpha * loudness[j]
     pulse_rates[j] = r0 * (1 - np.exp(-gamma * i))

     # Update the best position and fitness if improved
     if new_fitness < best_fitness:
      best_position = positions[j].copy()
      best_fitness = new_fitness
```

```python
    # Print the iteration number and the best fitness value
    print(f"Iteration {i+1}: Best fitness = {best_fitness:.4f}")

# Print the final result
print(f"Final result: Best solution = {best_position}, Best fitness =
{best_fitness:.4f}")
```

Cuckoo Search (CS)

- The 'ingredients' for the algorithm in the Recipe:
  - A population of cuckoos that can lay eggs in a continuous search space
  - A levy flight model that simulates the long-range jumps of the cuckoos
  - A discovery rate that determines how likely a host nest is to discover a cuckoo egg
  - A set of parameters that control the population size, the levy flight exponent, and the discovery rate

- An example of the recipe once it is 'cooked':
  - The CS can be used to find the optimal solution to a complex optimization problem, such as multimodal functions or engineering design
  - The CS starts with a random initialization of the cuckoo positions and fitness values
  - At each iteration, each cuckoo generates a new position by applying the levy flight model and evaluates its fitness value
  - If the new position has a better fitness value than its current one, the cuckoo replaces its position with the new one
  - A fraction of the worst cuckoos are abandoned and replaced by new ones randomly generated
  - The algorithm terminates when a predefined criterion is met, such as reaching a maximum number of iterations or achieving a desired solution quality

- A pseudocode Python example of the Recipe:

```python
Python
# Import numpy for numerical operations
import numpy as np

# Import scipy for levy flight generation
import scipy

# Define the fitness function (example: Michalewicz function)
def fitness(x):
    return -np.sum(np.sin(x) * np.sin((np.arange(1, len(x) + 1) * x**2) /
np.pi)**20)
```

```python
# Define the parameters of the CS
n_cuckoos = 100 # Number of cuckoos
n_dims = 10 # Number of dimensions
max_iter = 1000 # Maximum number of iterations
alpha = 0.01 # Levy flight scale factor
beta = 1.5 # Levy flight exponent
p = 0.25 # Discovery rate
lb = 0 # Lower bound of the search space
ub = np.pi # Upper bound of the search space

# Initialize the cuckoo positions and fitness values randomly
positions = np.random.uniform(lb, ub, (n_cuckoos, n_dims))
fitness_values = np.array([fitness(x) for x in positions])

# Find the best cuckoo position and its fitness value
best_position = positions[np.argmin(fitness_values)]
best_fitness = np.min(fitness_values)

# Main loop of the CS
for i in range(max_iter):
 # Loop over each cuckoo
 for j in range(n_cuckoos):
  # Generate a new position by applying the levy flight model
  new_position = positions[j] + alpha *
scipy.stats.levy_stable.rvs(beta, 0, size=n_dims)

  # Apply boundary conditions (clip the position to the search
space)
  new_position = np.clip(new_position, lb, ub)

  # Evaluate the fitness value of the new position
  new_fitness = fitness(new_position)

  # Compare the new fitness with the old one and update
accordingly
  if new_fitness < fitness_values[j]:
```

```python
        # Replace the old position and fitness with the new ones
        positions[j] = new_position.copy()
        fitness_values[j] = new_fitness

        # Update the best position and fitness if improved
        if new_fitness < best_fitness:
         best_position = positions[j].copy()
         best_fitness = new_fitness

     # Abandon a fraction of the worst cuckoos and replace them with
    new ones randomly generated
     n_abandoned = int(p * n_cuckoos)
     worst_indices = np.argsort(fitness_values)[-n_abandoned:]
     positions[worst_indices] = np.random.uniform(lb, ub, (n_abandoned,
    n_dims))
     fitness_values[worst_indices] = np.array([fitness(x) for x in
    positions[worst_indices]])

     # Print the iteration number and the best fitness value
     print(f"Iteration {i+1}: Best fitness = {best_fitness:.4f}")

    # Print the final result
    print(f"Final result: Best solution = {best_position}, Best fitness =
    {best_fitness:.4f}")
```

Whale Optimization Algorithm (WOA)

- The 'ingredients' for the algorithm in the Recipe:
  - A population of whales that can swim in a continuous search space
  - A spiral model that simulates the helical movement of the whales towards their prey
  - A encircling model that simulates the encircling behavior of the whales around their prey
  - A set of parameters that control the exploration and exploitation trade-off

- An example of the recipe once it is 'cooked':
  - The WOA can be used to find the optimal solution to a complex optimization problem, such as structural design or data clustering
  - The WOA starts with a random initialization of the whale positions and fitness values
  - At each iteration, each whale updates its position by applying either the spiral model or the encircling model, depending on a random parameter
  - The spiral model allows the whale to move towards the best solution in a spiral shape, while the encircling model allows the whale to move around the best solution randomly
  - The algorithm terminates when a predefined criterion is met, such as reaching a maximum number of iterations or achieving a desired solution quality

- A pseudocode Python example of the Recipe:

```python
Python
# Import numpy for numerical operations
import numpy as np

# Define the fitness function (example: Levy function)
def fitness(x):
  return np.sin(3 * np.pi * x[0])**2 + np.sum((x[:-1] - 1)**2 * (1 + 10 *
np.sin(np.pi * x[:-1] + 1)**2)) + (x[-1] - 1)**2 * (1 + np.sin(2 * np.pi
* x[-1])**2)

# Define the parameters of the WOA
n_whales = 100 # Number of whales
```

```python
n_dims = 10 # Number of dimensions
max_iter = 1000 # Maximum number of iterations
a_max = 2 # Maximum value of a parameter
a_min = 0 # Minimum value of a parameter
b = 1 # Constant for spiral model
lb = -10 # Lower bound of the search space
ub = 10 # Upper bound of the search space

# Initialize the whale positions and fitness values randomly
positions = np.random.uniform(lb, ub, (n_whales, n_dims))
fitness_values = np.array([fitness(x) for x in positions])

# Find the best whale position and its fitness value
best_position = positions[np.argmin(fitness_values)]
best_fitness = np.min(fitness_values)

# Main loop of the WOA
for i in range(max_iter):
 # Loop over each whale
 for j in range(n_whales):
  # Generate a random parameter between 0 and 1
  r = np.random.rand()

  # Update the value of a parameter linearly from a_max to a_min
  a = a_max - i * (a_max - a_min) / max_iter

  # Calculate the value of c parameter between -1 and 1
  c = 2 * r

  # Calculate the distance between the current whale and the best
whale
  d = np.abs(c * best_position - positions[j])

  # Choose either spiral model or encircling model based on a
random parameter p between 0 and 1
  p = np.random.rand()
```

```python
    if p < 0.5:
      # Use spiral model to update position
      l = np.random.uniform(-1, 1)
      new_position = d * np.exp(b * l) * np.cos(2 * np.pi * l) +
best_position

    else:
      # Use encircling model to update position
      new_position = best_position - a * d

    # Apply boundary conditions (clip the position to the search
space)
    new_position = np.clip(new_position, lb, ub)

    # Evaluate the fitness value of the new position
    new_fitness = fitness(new_position)

    # Compare the new fitness with the old one and update
accordingly
    if new_fitness < fitness_values[j]:
      # Replace the old position and fitness with the new ones
      positions[j] = new_position.copy()
      fitness_values[j] = new_fitness

      # Update the best position and fitness if improved
      if new_fitness < best_fitness:
       best_position = positions[j].copy()
       best_fitness = new_fitness

  # Print the iteration number and the best fitness value
  print(f"Iteration {i+1}: Best fitness = {best_fitness:.4f}")

# Print the final result
print(f"Final result: Best solution = {best_position}, Best fitness =
{best_fitness:.4f}")
```

Flower Pollination Algorithm (FPA)

- The 'ingredients' for the algorithm in the Recipe:
  - A population of flowers that can pollinate in a continuous search space
  - A global pollination model that simulates the long-distance movement of pollen by wind or insects
  - A local pollination model that simulates the short-distance movement of pollen by self-pollination or biotic pollination
  - A set of parameters that control the switching probability between global and local pollination, and the step size of the pollination

- An example of the recipe once it is 'cooked':
  - The FPA can be used to find the optimal solution to a complex optimization problem, such as multimodal functions or engineering design
  - The FPA starts with a random initialization of the flower positions and fitness values
  - At each iteration, each flower generates a new position by applying either the global pollination model or the local pollination model, depending on a random parameter
  - The global pollination model allows the flower to move towards the best solution in a levy flight fashion, while the local pollination model allows the flower to move around its current solution randomly
  - The algorithm terminates when a predefined criterion is met, such as reaching a maximum number of iterations or achieving a desired solution quality

- A pseudocode Python example of the Recipe:

```python
Python
# Import numpy for numerical operations
import numpy as np

# Import scipy for levy flight generation
import scipy

# Define the fitness function (example: Easom function)
def fitness(x):
```

```python
    return -np.cos(x[0]) * np.cos(x[1]) * np.exp(-((x[0] - np.pi)**2 +
(x[1] - np.pi)**2))

# Define the parameters of the FPA
n_flowers = 100 # Number of flowers
n_dims = 2 # Number of dimensions
max_iter = 1000 # Maximum number of iterations
p = 0.8 # Switching probability between global and local
pollination
gamma = 0.1 # Step size factor for global pollination
lb = -100 # Lower bound of the search space
ub = 100 # Upper bound of the search space

# Initialize the flower positions and fitness values randomly
positions = np.random.uniform(lb, ub, (n_flowers, n_dims))
fitness_values = np.array([fitness(x) for x in positions])

# Find the best flower position and its fitness value
best_position = positions[np.argmin(fitness_values)]
best_fitness = np.min(fitness_values)

# Main loop of the FPA
for i in range(max_iter):
 # Loop over each flower
 for j in range(n_flowers):
  # Choose either global pollination or local pollination based
on a random parameter q between 0 and 1
  q = np.random.rand()

  if q < p:
   # Use global pollination to update position
   new_position = positions[j] + gamma *
scipy.stats.levy_stable.rvs(1.5, 0, size=n_dims) * (best_position -
positions[j])

  else:
   # Use local pollination to update position
```

```python
    # Choose a random neighbor index (different from j)
    neighbor = j
    while neighbor == j:
      neighbor = np.random.randint(n_flowers)

    # Generate a new position by adding some randomness to current
position and neighbor position difference
    new_position = positions[j] + np.random.uniform(-1, 1, n_dims) *
(positions[j] - positions[neighbor])

   # Apply boundary conditions (clip the position to the search
space)
   new_position = np.clip(new_position, lb, ub)

   # Evaluate the fitness value of the new position
   new_fitness = fitness(new_position)

   # Compare the new fitness with the old one and update
accordingly
   if new_fitness < fitness_values[j]:
    # Replace the old position and fitness with the new ones
    positions[j] = new_position.copy()
    fitness_values[j] = new_fitness

    # Update the best position and fitness if improved
    if new_fitness < best_fitness:
     best_position = positions[j].copy()
     best_fitness = new_fitness

 # Print the iteration number and the best fitness value
 print(f"Iteration {i+1}: Best fitness = {best_fitness:.4f}")

# Print the final result
print(f"Final result: Best solution = {best_position}, Best fitness =
{best_fitness:.4f}")
```

Moth Flame Optimization (MFO)

- The 'ingredients' for the algorithm in the Recipe:
  - A population of moths that are attracted to flames in a search space
  - Flames that represent solutions in the search space
  - A spiral equation to model the moths' movement around a flame
  - Multiple flame number and flame absorption coefficients to alternate between exploration and exploitation

- An example of the recipe once it is 'cooked':
  - The MFO can optimize complex problems like classification, clustering, scheduling, etc.
  - It starts by initializing the moth population randomly and evaluating their fitness
  - The best moth is chosen as the first flame source
  - At each iteration, moths update their position using the spiral equation around a flame
  - Flames are updated by better moth solutions found during the iteration
  - The algorithm balances exploration vs exploitation by adjusting the flames and their absorption coefficients
  - It terminates when the maximum iterations are reached

- A pseudocode Python example of the Recipe:

```Python
# Import numpy for numerical operations
import numpy as np

# Import scipy for levy flight generation
import scipy

# Define the fitness function (example: Easom function)
def fitness(x):
  return -np.cos(x[0]) * np.cos(x[1]) * np.exp(-((x[0] - np.pi)**2 +
(x[1] - np.pi)**2))

# Define the parameters of the MFO
n_moths = 100 # Number of moths
n_dims = 2 # Number of dimensions
max_iter = 1000 # Maximum number of iterations
gamma = 0.1 # Step size factor for spiral equation
lb = -100 # Lower bound of the search space
```

```python
ub = 100 # Upper bound of the search space

# Initialize the moth positions and fitness values randomly
positions = np.random.uniform(lb, ub, (n_moths, n_dims))
fitness_values = np.array([fitness(x) for x in positions])

# Find the best moth position and its fitness value
best_position = positions[np.argmin(fitness_values)]
best_fitness = np.min(fitness_values)

# Initialize the flame positions and fitness values as copies of
the best moth position and fitness value
flames = np.tile(best_position, (n_moths, 1))
flame_fitness = np.tile(best_fitness, n_moths)

# Main loop of the MFO
for i in range(max_iter):
 # Loop over each moth
 for j in range(n_moths):
  # Choose a random flame index
  flame_index = np.random.randint(n_moths)

  # Calculate the distance between the current moth and the
chosen flame
  distance = np.linalg.norm(positions[j] - flames[flame_index])

  # Generate a new position by applying the spiral equation
around the chosen flame
  new_position = distance * np.exp(-gamma * distance) * np.cos(2 *
np.pi * distance) + flames[flame_index]

  # Apply boundary conditions (clip the position to the search
space)
  new_position = np.clip(new_position, lb, ub)

  # Evaluate the fitness value of the new position
  new_fitness = fitness(new_position)
```

```python
        # Compare the new fitness with the old one and update
accordingly
        if new_fitness < fitness_values[j]:
            # Replace the old position and fitness with the new ones
            positions[j] = new_position.copy()
            fitness_values[j] = new_fitness

            # Update the best position and fitness if improved
            if new_fitness < best_fitness:
                best_position = positions[j].copy()
                best_fitness = new_fitness

    # Sort the moths by their fitness values in ascending order
    sorted_indices = np.argsort(fitness_values)
    positions = positions[sorted_indices]
    fitness_values = fitness_values[sorted_indices]

    # Update the number of flames based on a linear decreasing
scheme
    n_flames = n_moths - i * (n_moths - 1) // max_iter

    # Update the flame positions and fitness values by copying from
the best moths
    flames[:n_flames] = positions[:n_flames].copy()
    flame_fitness[:n_flames] = fitness_values[:n_flames].copy()

    # Print the iteration number and the best fitness value
    print(f"Iteration {i+1}: Best fitness = {best_fitness:.4f}")

# Print the final result
print(f"Final result: Best solution = {best_position}, Best fitness =
{best_fitness:.4f}")
```

Grey Wolf Optimizer (GWO)

- The 'ingredients' for the algorithm in the Recipe:
- ○ A population of grey wolves that can hunt in a continuous search space
- ○ A leader wolf (alpha) that guides the pack towards promising areas
- ○ Follower wolves (beta and delta) that help scout the search space
- ○ Omega wolves that follow the guidance of the alpha, beta and delta wolves
- ○ A set of encircling, hunting, and attacking coefficients to balance exploration vs exploitation

- An example of the recipe once it is 'cooked':
- ○ The GWO can be used to find the optimal solution to complex optimization problems like function optimization, feature selection, scheduling, etc.
- ○ The GWO starts by randomly initializing the grey wolf population
- ○ At each iteration, the alpha, beta, and delta wolves guide the omega wolves by updating their distance and position based on the best three solutions
- ○ The omega wolves update their positions by encircling, hunting, and attacking the prey guided by the top three wolves
- ○ The algorithm terminates when it reaches the maximum iterations or an acceptable solution

- A pseudocode Python example of the Recipe:

```Python
# Import numpy for numerical operations
import numpy as np

# Define the fitness function (example: Easom function)
def fitness(x):
  return -np.cos(x[0]) * np.cos(x[1]) * np.exp(-((x[0] - np.pi)**2 +
(x[1] - np.pi)**2))

# Define the parameters of the GWO
n_wolves = 100 # Number of wolves
n_dims = 2 # Number of dimensions
max_iter = 1000 # Maximum number of iterations
A1 = 2 # Parameter for encircling prey
A2 = 2 # Parameter for encircling prey
A3 = 2 # Parameter for encircling prey
A4 = 2 # Parameter for attacking prey
lb = -100 # Lower bound of the search space
```

```python
ub = 100 # Upper bound of the search space

# Initialize the wolf positions and fitness values randomly
positions = np.random.uniform(lb, ub, (n_wolves, n_dims))
fitness_values = np.array([fitness(x) for x in positions])

# Find the best wolf position and its fitness value
best_position = positions[np.argmin(fitness_values)]
best_fitness = np.min(fitness_values)

# Main loop of the GWO
for i in range(max_iter):
 # Loop over each wolf
 for j in range(n_wolves):
  # Choose a random alpha, beta, and delta wolf from the
population
   alpha, beta, delta = np.random.choice(n_wolves, size=3,
replace=False)

   # Calculate the distance between the current wolf and the
alpha, beta, and delta wolves
   D_alpha = np.linalg.norm(positions[j] - positions[alpha])
   D_beta = np.linalg.norm(positions[j] - positions[beta])
   D_delta = np.linalg.norm(positions[j] - positions[delta])

   # Generate a new position by encircling the alpha, beta, and
delta wolves
   X1 = positions[alpha] - A1 * D_alpha * np.random.rand()
   X2 = positions[beta] - A2 * D_beta * np.random.rand()
   X3 = positions[delta] - A3 * D_delta * np.random.rand()

   # Generate a new position by hunting the average position of
the three wolves
   X_hunt = (X1 + X2 + X3) / 3

   # Generate a new position by attacking the alpha wolf with some
randomness
```

```python
    X_attack = X_hunt - A4 * (np.random.rand() - 0.5) * D_alpha

    # Apply boundary conditions (clip the position to the search
space)
    X_attack = np.clip(X_attack, lb, ub)

    # Evaluate the fitness value of the new position
    new_fitness = fitness(X_attack)

    # Compare the new fitness with the old one and update
accordingly
    if new_fitness < fitness_values[j]:
     # Replace the old position and fitness with the new ones
     positions[j] = X_attack.copy()
     fitness_values[j] = new_fitness

     # Update the best position and fitness if improved
     if new_fitness < best_fitness:
      best_position = positions[j].copy()
      best_fitness = new_fitness

  # Print the iteration number and the best fitness value
  print(f"Iteration {i+1}: Best fitness = {best_fitness:.4f}")

# Print the final result
print(f"Final result: Best solution = {best_position}, Best fitness =
{best_fitness:.4f}")
```

Penguin Optimization Algorithm (POA)

- The 'ingredients' for the algorithm in the Recipe:
    - A population of penguins that can dive and swim in a continuous search space
    - A prey matrix that stores the position and fitness value of each prey (a potential solution)
    - A diving model that simulates the penguins' movement towards the prey
    - A swimming model that simulates the penguins' movement around the prey
    - A set of parameters that control the diving depth, the swimming radius, and the number of prey

- An example of the recipe once it is 'cooked':
    - The POA can be used to find the optimal solution to a complex optimization problem, such as multimodal functions or engineering design
    - The POA starts with a random initialization of the penguin positions and fitness values
    - The best penguin is chosen as the first prey source
    - At each iteration, each penguin updates its position by applying either the diving model or the swimming model, depending on a random parameter
    - The diving model allows the penguin to move towards the best solution in a spiral shape, while the swimming model allows the penguin to move around the best solution randomly
    - The prey are updated by better penguin solutions found during the iteration
    - The algorithm terminates when a predefined criterion is met, such as reaching a maximum number of iterations or finding a satisfactory solution

- A pseudocode Python example of the Recipe:

```python
# Import numpy for numerical operations
import numpy as np

# Define the fitness function (example: Easom function)
def fitness(x):
  return -np.cos(x[0]) * np.cos(x[1]) * np.exp(-((x[0] - np.pi)**2 + (x[1] - np.pi)**2))

# Define the parameters of the POA
n_penguins = 100 # Number of penguins
n_dims = 2 # Number of dimensions
max_iter = 1000 # Maximum number of iterations
alpha = 0.01 # Diving depth factor
```

```python
beta = 0.1 # Swimming radius factor
p = 0.5 # Switching probability between diving and swimming
lb = -100 # Lower bound of the search space
ub = 100 # Upper bound of the search space

# Initialize the penguin positions and fitness values randomly
positions = np.random.uniform(lb, ub, (n_penguins, n_dims))
fitness_values = np.array([fitness(x) for x in positions])

# Find the best penguin position and its fitness value
best_position = positions[np.argmin(fitness_values)]
best_fitness = np.min(fitness_values)

# Initialize the prey positions and fitness values as copies of the best penguin position and
fitness value
prey = np.tile(best_position, (n_penguins, 1))
prey_fitness = np.tile(best_fitness, n_penguins)

# Main loop of the POA
for i in range(max_iter):
  # Loop over each penguin
  for j in range(n_penguins):
    # Choose a random prey index
    prey_index = np.random.randint(n_penguins)

    # Calculate the distance between the current penguin and the chosen prey
    distance = np.linalg.norm(positions[j] - prey[prey_index])

    # Choose either diving model or swimming model based on a random parameter q between 0
and 1
    q = np.random.rand()

    if q < p:
      # Use diving model to update position
      new_position = distance * np.exp(-alpha * distance) * np.cos(2 * np.pi * distance) +
prey[prey_index]

    else:
      # Use swimming model to update position
      new_position = prey[prey_index] + beta * distance * np.random.uniform(-1, 1, n_dims)

    # Apply boundary conditions (clip the position to the search space)
    new_position = np.clip(new_position, lb, ub)
```

```python
    # Evaluate the fitness value of the new position
    new_fitness = fitness(new_position)

    # Compare the new fitness with the old one and update accordingly
    if new_fitness < fitness_values[j]:
      # Replace the old position and fitness with the new ones
      positions[j] = new_position.copy()
      fitness_values[j] = new_fitness

      # Update the best position and fitness if improved
      if new_fitness < best_fitness:
        best_position = positions[j].copy()
        best_fitness = new_fitness

  # Sort the penguins by their fitness values in ascending order
  sorted_indices = np.argsort(fitness_values)
  positions = positions[sorted_indices]
  fitness_values = fitness_values[sorted_indices]

  # Update the number of prey based on a linear decreasing scheme
  n_prey = n_penguins - i * (n_penguins - 1) // max_iter

  # Update the prey positions and fitness values by copying from the best penguins
  prey[:n_prey] = positions[:n_prey].copy()
  prey_fitness[:n_prey] = fitness_values[:n_prey].copy()

  # Print the iteration number and the best fitness value
  print(f"Iteration {i+1}: Best fitness = {best_fitness:.4f}")

# Print the final result
print(f"Final result: Best solution = {best_position}, Best fitness = {best_fitness:.4f}")
```

Honey Badger Optimization Algorithm (HBOA)

- The 'ingredients' for the algorithm in the Recipe:
  - A population of honey badgers that can dig and hunt in a continuous search space
  - A food source matrix that stores the position and fitness value of each food source (a potential solution)
  - A digging model that simulates the honey badgers' movement towards the food sources
  - A hunting model that simulates the honey badgers' movement around the food sources
  - A set of parameters that control the digging depth, the hunting radius, and the number of food sources

- An example of the recipe once it is 'cooked':
  - The HBOA can be used to find the optimal solution to a complex optimization problem, such as multimodal functions or engineering design
  - The HBOA starts with a random initialization of the honey badger positions and fitness values
  - The best honey badger is chosen as the first food source
  - At each iteration, each honey badger updates its position by applying either the digging model or the hunting model, depending on a random parameter
  - The digging model allows the honey badger to move towards the best solution in a spiral shape, while the hunting model allows the honey badger to move around the best solution randomly
  - The food sources are updated by better honey badger solutions found during the iteration
  - The algorithm terminates when a predefined criterion is met, such as reaching a maximum number of iterations or finding a satisfactory solution

- A pseudocode Python example of the Recipe:

```python
# Import numpy for numerical operations
import numpy as np

# Define the fitness function (example: Easom function)
def fitness(x):
  return -np.cos(x[0]) * np.cos(x[1]) * np.exp(-((x[0] - np.pi)**2 + (x[1] - np.pi)**2))

# Define the parameters of the HBOA
```

```python
n_badgers = 100 # Number of honey badgers
n_dims = 2 # Number of dimensions
max_iter = 1000 # Maximum number of iterations
alpha = 0.01 # Digging depth factor
beta = 0.1 # Hunting radius factor
p = 0.5 # Switching probability between digging and hunting
lb = -100 # Lower bound of the search space
ub = 100 # Upper bound of the search space

# Initialize the honey badger positions and fitness values randomly
positions = np.random.uniform(lb, ub, (n_badgers, n_dims))
fitness_values = np.array([fitness(x) for x in positions])

# Find the best honey badger position and its fitness value
best_position = positions[np.argmin(fitness_values)]
best_fitness = np.min(fitness_values)

# Initialize the food source positions and fitness values as copies of the best honey badger
position and fitness value
food_sources = np.tile(best_position, (n_badgers, 1))
food_fitness = np.tile(best_fitness, n_badgers)

# Main loop of the HBOA
for i in range(max_iter):
  # Loop over each honey badger
  for j in range(n_badgers):
    # Choose a random food source index
    food_index = np.random.randint(n_badgers)

    # Calculate the distance between the current honey badger and the chosen food source
    distance = np.linalg.norm(positions[j] - food_sources[food_index])

    # Choose either digging model or hunting model based on a random parameter q between 0
and 1
    q = np.random.rand()

    if q < p:
      # Use digging model to update position
      new_position = distance * np.exp(-alpha * distance) * np.cos(2 * np.pi * distance) +
food_sources[food_index]

    else:
      # Use hunting model to update position
```

```python
        new_position = food_sources[food_index] + beta * distance * np.random.uniform(-1, 1,
n_dims)

        # Apply boundary conditions (clip the position to the search space)
        new_position = np.clip(new_position, lb, ub)

        # Evaluate the fitness value of the new position
        new_fitness = fitness(new_position)

        # Compare the new fitness with the old one and update accordingly
        if new_fitness < fitness_values[j]:
          # Replace the old position and fitness with the new ones
          positions[j] = new_position.copy()
          fitness_values[j] = new_fitness

          # Update the best position and fitness if improved
          if new_fitness < best_fitness:
            best_position = positions[j].copy()
            best_fitness = new_fitness

      # Sort the honey badgers by their fitness values in ascending order
      sorted_indices = np.argsort(fitness_values)
      positions = positions[sorted_indices]
      fitness_values = fitness_values[sorted_indices]

      # Update the number of food sources based on a linear decreasing scheme
      n_food = n_badgers - i * (n_badgers - 1) // max_iter

      # Update the food source positions and fitness values by copying from the best honey badgers
      food_sources[:n_food] = positions[:n_food].copy()
      food_fitness[:n_food] = fitness_values[:n_food].copy()

      # Print the iteration number and the best fitness value
      print(f"Iteration {i+1}: Best fitness = {best_fitness:.4f}")

    # Print the final result
    print(f"Final result: Best solution = {best_position}, Best fitness = {best_fitness:.4f}")
```

Octopus Optimization Algorithm (OOA)

- The 'ingredients' for the algorithm in the Recipe:

    - A population of octopuses that can change color and shape in a continuous search space
    - A camouflage matrix that stores the position and fitness value of each camouflage (a potential solution)
    - A color change model that simulates the octopuses' ability to match their color to their surroundings
    - A shape change model that simulates the octopuses' ability to alter their body shape and texture to mimic other objects or animals
    - A set of parameters that control the color change rate, the shape change rate, and the number of camouflages

- An example of the recipe once it is 'cooked':
    - The OOA can be used to find the optimal solution to a complex optimization problem, such as multimodal functions or engineering design
    - The OOA starts with a random initialization of the octopus positions and fitness values
    - The best octopus is chosen as the first camouflage source
    - At each iteration, each octopus updates its position by applying either the color change model or the shape change model, depending on a random parameter
    - The color change model allows the octopus to move towards the best solution in a levy flight fashion, while the shape change model allows the octopus to move around the best solution randomly
    - The camouflages are updated by better octopus solutions found during the iteration
    - The algorithm terminates when a predefined criterion is met, such as reaching a maximum number of iterations or finding a satisfactory solution

- A pseudocode Python example of the Recipe:

```python
# Import numpy for numerical operations
import numpy as np

# Import scipy for levy flight generation
import scipy
```

```python
# Define the fitness function (example: Easom function)
def fitness(x):
  return -np.cos(x[0]) * np.cos(x[1]) * np.exp(-((x[0] - np.pi)**2 + (x[1] - np.pi)**2))

# Define the parameters of the OOA
n_octopuses = 100 # Number of octopuses
n_dims = 2 # Number of dimensions
max_iter = 1000 # Maximum number of iterations
alpha = 0.01 # Color change rate factor
beta = 0.1 # Shape change rate factor
p = 0.5 # Switching probability between color change and shape change
lb = -100 # Lower bound of the search space
ub = 100 # Upper bound of the search space

# Initialize the octopus positions and fitness values randomly
positions = np.random.uniform(lb, ub, (n_octopuses, n_dims))
fitness_values = np.array([fitness(x) for x in positions])

# Find the best octopus position and its fitness value
best_position = positions[np.argmin(fitness_values)]
best_fitness = np.min(fitness_values)

# Initialize the camouflage positions and fitness values as copies of the best octopus position
and fitness value
camouflages = np.tile(best_position, (n_octopuses, 1))
camouflage_fitness = np.tile(best_fitness, n_octopuses)

# Main loop of the OOA
for i in range(max_iter):
  # Loop over each octopus
  for j in range(n_octopuses):
    # Choose a random camouflage index
    camouflage_index = np.random.randint(n_octopuses)

    # Calculate the distance between the current octopus and the chosen camouflage
    distance = np.linalg.norm(positions[j] - camouflages[camouflage_index])

    # Choose either color change model or shape change model based on a random parameter q
between 0 and 1
    q = np.random.rand()

    if q < p:
      # Use color change model to update position
```

```python
            new_position = positions[j] + alpha * scipy.stats.levy_stable.rvs(1.5, 0, size=n_dims) * \
(camouflages[camouflage_index] - positions[j])

        else:
            # Use shape change model to update position
            new_position = camouflages[camouflage_index] + beta * distance * np.random.uniform(-1,
1, n_dims)

        # Apply boundary conditions (clip the position to the search space)
        new_position = np.clip(new_position, lb, ub)

        # Evaluate the fitness value of the new position
        new_fitness = fitness(new_position)

        # Compare the new fitness with the old one and update accordingly
        if new_fitness < fitness_values[j]:
            # Replace the old position and fitness with the new ones
            positions[j] = new_position.copy()
            fitness_values[j] = new_fitness

            # Update the best position and fitness if improved
            if new_fitness < best_fitness:
                best_position = positions[j].copy()
                best_fitness = new_fitness

    # Sort the octopuses by their fitness values in ascending order
    sorted_indices = np.argsort(fitness_values)
    positions = positions[sorted_indices]
    fitness_values = fitness_values[sorted_indices]

    # Update the number of camouflages based on a linear decreasing scheme
    n_camouflages = n_octopuses - i * (n_octopuses - 1) // max_iter

    # Update the camouflage positions and fitness values by copying from the best octopuses
    camouflages[:n_camouflages] = positions[:n_camouflages].copy()
    camouflage_fitness[:n_camouflages] = fitness_values[:n_camouflages].copy()

    # Print the iteration number and the best fitness value
    print(f"Iteration {i+1}: Best fitness = {best_fitness:.4f}")

# Print the final result
# print(f"Final result: Best solution = {best_position}, Best fitness = {best_fitness:.4f}")
```

www.ingramcontent.com/pod-product-compliance
Lightning Source LLC
Chambersburg PA
CBHW061052050326
40690CB00012B/2593